THE A OF

HADRIAN'S WALL

by

BRIAN DOBSON and DAVID J. BREEZE

© 1972

SBN 902833 76 6

Northern History Booklets No. 28

Published by Frank Graham, 6 Queen's Terrace, Newcastle upon Tyne NE2 2PL
Printed by J. & P. Bealls Ltd., Gallowgate, Newcastle upon Tyne NE1 4SA

We would like to thank Dr. D. J. Smith for his advice and encouragement in the writing of this booklet, Mr. Frank Graham for his friendly help, particularly with the illustrations, Miss Mary M. Hurrell for drawing the maps, plans and weapons, Dr. N. McCord and the University of Newcastle upon Tyne for permission to use the air photographs, and the Museum of Antiquities of the University and the Society of Antiquaries of Newcastle upon Tyne for the majority of the other illustrations.

BRIAN DOBSON
DAVID J. BREEZE

The front cover shows an artist's impression of the South Gate of Housesteads Fort and the adjacent part of the civil settlement in the third century A.D. It is based on the reconstruction of the West Gate by I. A. Richmond and F. A. Child.

THE ARMY OF HADRIAN'S WALL

Introduction

Most people's first reaction to the army of Hadrian's Wall is one of sympathy. As they stand on Housesteads on a typical day they sigh, "What a change from Italy for the Romans", visualising legionaries born in Italy shipped off to the rigours of the Wall. However, their reaction is based on two common misconceptions: that the Wall was manned by the legions and that the soldiers of Rome were always exclusively recruited from Italy. To combat these and other errors and to give an account of what is known about the army of the Wall is the purpose of this handbook.

Any general account of the Roman army must begin with a description of the organisation of the various units and the way they evolved. This is covered in the first section. The second section considers how the officers and men were recruited and trained: their homes, social background and prospects of promotion. Life on the Wall itself is described in the third section, with a close linking of the lay-out and visible buildings of the forts and the various aspects of the life on and off duty of officers and men which they reflect: pay, duties, leisure, marriage, retirement, death and burial, beliefs and superstitions.

The Wall was garrisoned, apart from two periods in the second century, from the 120's to the early 400's. During this time there was considerable change in the organisation of the army, particularly under the stresses of the third century. By the early fourth century cavalry had become the dominant arm, and mobile field armies behind the frontier lines were of higher quality and greater importance than the troops actually stationed on the frontier, so that the aspects of military life treated in the first three chapters changed almost beyond recognition. Our knowledge of these changes, in particular as they affected the army of the Wall, is slight, and as yet no coherent account can be given of them. To meet this difficulty the terms of reference of the descriptive chapters are limited, so that it is basically the army of the Wall as it was from the 120's A.D. to around 250 that is described, with no account being taken of the far-reaching changes that were probably introduced into this province on the lines of developments elsewhere in the early fourth century. A brief epilogue touches on these changes.

One thing does remain constant. The units on the Wall must have been reorganised as a result of the changes referred to above, but they kept their old names, so that the units first identified on the Wall in the early third century were still surviving there in the fifth, as the *Notitia Dignitatum*, a surviving document which appears to be an official Roman one of that date, shows. These Wall regiments with what is known of their history appear in the last section.

THE ORGANISATION OF THE ARMY

The Roman army began its existence as the citizen body in arms, led by its king or later its elected magistrates, armed as well as individuals could afford to equip themselves. There is no space here to follow through in detail the stages in the development of this force, indistinguishable from others of its period, into the legions. By the time of Julius Caesar, in the mid-first century B.C., these were units of heavy infantrymen with armour that afforded them complete protection of the head and body with, as offensive weapons, the javelin (*pilum*) that killed the man or rendered the shield useless and the short stabbing sword (*gladius*) which they wielded with a mastery made possible by constant practice; men who were held together and controlled by iron discipline.

The legion thus specialised in the role of heavy infantry was decisive in the set-piece battle. But the disappearance in the process of earlier lighter-armed elements and the reduction of cavalry to a body of 120 men in each legion created problems. Without cavalry the enemy could not be pursued and a retreat turned into a rout. This is most vividly illustrated in the story of Caesar in Britain, when his cavalry failed to accompany him and he was considerably handicapped in pursuing his mobile foes.

It is not surprising therefore that already under the Roman Republic men accustomed to fight from horseback were being recruited from inside and outside the Roman Empire. At first they fought in their traditional dress and equipment, under their own leaders, but in the late Republic and early Principate these horsemen were formed into regular units (*alae*).

The need for infantry in addition to the legions also made itself felt. Apart from specialists such as archers and slingers ordinary infantrymen were recruited, as the horsemen had been. At first at least their role was not so important as that of the cavalry, and they were not so quickly formed into regular units. By the 70's A.D. they had been so organised, in *cohortes*, and with the *alae* were capable of bearing the main burden of fighting, freeing the legions for use as a tactical reserve and corps of engineers, though the legions still remained the decisive force in the big set-piece encounters. It was perhaps as a result of this development that a larger size of both *ala* and cohort appeared, the milliary cohort in the late 70's and the milliary *ala* still later but before the end of the first century A.D. These formed bigger units to use in the place of the legion in the line of battle.

A curious and imperfectly understood type of unit is the *cohors equitata*, the infantry regiment with a cavalry element. The temptation to speak of these as mounted infantry must be avoided. Mounted infantry dismount to fight; these *equites cohortales* were cavalry, though second-class cavalry. In battle or when armies were on the march they were brigaded with the cavalry; for units stationed on frontier lines they provided extended range for patrol work. The first such units appeared under Augustus; *cohortes equitatae* of milliary size appear at the same time as the other milliary cohorts.

All these units were based on the *centuria*, the infantry century commanded by a centurion, and the *turma*, the cavalry troop, commanded by a decurion.

Their organisation seems to have been modelled on that of the legion. The legion was divided into ten cohorts, the first containing five double centuries, the other nine cohorts six centuries each. This is the pattern reflected in the barrack accommodation at Inchtuthil, the short-lived legionary fortress built in Perthshire in the 80's. Other evidence suggests that legionary centuries were eighty men strong. The ordinary auxiliary infantry cohort was of six centuries, and seems to be based on the legionary cohorts II-X. The milliary cohort had ten centuries, paralleling and probably derived from the first cohort of the legion. The question arises what was the strength of the centuries in the auxiliary units. Some have held that in the milliary cohorts it was one hundred, to justify the term *milliaria* (one thousand strong) but it seems preferable to suppose that the century strength was kept the same throughout, at eighty, giving an ordinary auxiliary cohort a strength of 480 men (they were called *quingenariae*, equals five hundred strong) and milliary cohorts a strength of 800 men, like the first cohort of the legion, which was also called milliary. There is no decisive evidence either way.

The *ala* seems also to have consisted of 480 men, the same number as in the legionary and auxiliary quingenary cohorts. It was a multiple of the legionary cavalry force of 120 men, but unlike the legionary cavalry it was organised into *turmae*, commanded by decurions. The number in each of the sixteen *turmae* of the ordinary *ala* (also termed *quingenaria*) is estimated as thirty, or thirty-two if the two junior officers are included.

The organisation of the milliary *ala*, the rarest of the units of the Roman army, poses a difficult problem. It had twenty-four *turmae*, one and a half times as many as the quingenary *ala*. Did the *turmae* have the same strength as in the quingenary *ala*, giving a paper strength of 720 or 768, for which the description as milliary might seem inappropriate, or was the *turma* strength in milliary *alae* increased to say forty-two, to give a paper strength of 1,008? Again, there is no means of deciding at present.

The mixed units, the *cohortes equitatae*, were composed of six centuries and four *turmae* (*quingenariae*) and ten centuries and eight *turmae* (*milliariae*) respectively. The problem here is slightly different but also hinges on whether the term quingenary and milliary were precisely accurate and whether the paper strength of centuries and *turmae* was or was not constant throughout these different types of unit. A *cohors quingenaria equitata* may have been 480 infantry plus 120 cavalry (600 men) or it may be felt that the infantry should have been reduced in number to 360 (sixty a century) to keep the total at 480. A *cohors milliaria equitata* is acceptable as 800 infantry plus 240 cavalry (1,040 men). There is no difficulty here in fact if the assumption is

5

that the cavalry were additional to 800 infantry; if the working assumption is that a milliary infantry cohort must have ten centuries of 100 men then it must be assumed that the centuries were reduced in size from 100 to eighty when the unit became *equitata*.

All these rather complicated alternatives are summarised in the table below. The figures in brackets are those suggested by scholars who feel that quingenary and milliary must be interpreted in an absolute sense in every case.

ROMAN MILITARY ORGANISATION – UNIT STRENGTH

Unit	centuriae	men per centuria	total	turmae	men per turma	total	grand total
cohors legionis II-X	6	80	480				480
cohors auxiliaris quingenaria (D)	6	80	480				480
cohors auxiliaris (D) equitata	6	80 (60)	480 (360)	4	30	120	600 (480)
cohors legionis prima milliaria	5 double	80	800				800
cohors auxiliaris milliaria	10	80 (100)	800 (1000)				800 (1000)
cohors auxiliaris M equitata	10	80	800	8	30	240	1040
equites legionis						120	120
ala quingenaria				16	30	480	480
ala milliaria				24	30 (42)	720	720 (1008)

The legions and the *alae* and *cohortes* were not the only units in the Roman army. There were also the *numeri*. The *numerus*, a word which simply meant unit, in the second and third century was used to designate a unit which was not an *ala* or a cohort. Such units had their own widely varying internal organisation and were raised for special purposes.

The fleets (*classes*) do not come into the province of this handbook, though it will be recalled that a detachment of the British fleet built a granary at Benwell. They were organised differently, by ships and squadrons of ships. The troops stationed in Rome, i.e. the emperor's guards (*cohortes praetoriae*), Rome police (*cohortes urbanae*), and fire service (*cohortes vigilum*) were organised in cohorts and centuries, but as units are not relevant to the Wall.

On the Wall, while it was by and large the legions which carried out the skilled work of construction, it was the *alae* and *cohortes* which formed the garrison. In a later chapter the extent to which the visible remains of the forts on the Wall reflect the organisation and routine of these units will be considered.

OFFICERS AND MEN

Under the Republic the consuls had succeeded the king as supreme in peace and war. Under them the legions as they evolved were commanded by six *tribuni militum*, serving in pairs by rota. In the late Republic Pompey and Caesar in particular employed the device of appointing deputies, *legati*, to command legions and perform other functions. Under the emperors the imperial provinces, those which they directly controlled as super-magistrates (their constitutional position in theory), were governed through *legati Augusti pro praetore*, while the legions were commanded by simple *legati Augusti*. Of the six tribunates one post, later known as that of the *tribunus laticlavius*, became senior and was reserved, as were the posts as *legati*, for the old aristocracy, the senate. It is not possible here to go further into the background and training of these officers, except to observe that as command in war was regarded as a corollary of rule in peace no special military training was ever envisaged, since it was assumed that those who could be trusted to do the one job could do the other. The career of the senator contained both civil and military posts, culminating in posts as governor which involved both command of the army in the province and full administrative responsibility for the civil population.

Beneath the senators, who belonged to a body far older than the emperors, which could trace its origins back to the days of the kings and had ruled most of the world the Romans knew for centuries, were the equestrians. They were men who had a property qualification (400,000 sesterces) and were free born and of blameless reputation. Under the Republic their role in public affairs had been very restricted in terms of official posts, but the emperors put their talents to considerable use. They filled the other five posts in the legionary tribunate; they were the *tribuni angusticlavii*, the men who wore on their tunic the narrow purple stripe, as distinct from the broad stripe of the *laticlavius*, the future senator (technically a man was not a senator by birth; he became one on entering the senate, generally as *quaestor*).

When the cavalry and infantry that had been recruited to fulfil duties which were impossible or undesirable for the legions were being formed into regular units, with standardised organisation and equipment, commanders for them were taken from a variety of sources: legionary centurions, tribal leaders, equestrians. After about A.D. 70 other sources were rarely used, and it was the equestrians who supplied the commanding officers of *alae* and *cohortes* for the period with which we are concerned, A.D. 120-250, though towards the end of the period the supply was being supplemented by men who had risen from the ranks of the legions or the guard.

These equestrian officers were recruited from all over the Empire, not only Italy, Spain and Gaul (France) but from North Africa and the Middle East. They emerged often from families that were dominant in the towns, the municipal aristocracies which supplied the magistrates and town councillors who did much of the work of running the Empire at the self-governing city level. Some were young men, in their twenties, but the majority had served as senior magistrates in their home towns and entered military service in their thirties. By the time of Hadrian it was customary to begin service with a post as *praefectus cohortis*, commander of a quingenary cohort. There were some 270 posts of this nature around the middle of the second century. After a period of perhaps three years in this post the equestrian might hope for a post in a legion as *tribunus angusticlavius*, or as tribune of a milliary cohort. Commanders of milliary cohorts were normally called tribunes, though there were exceptions; the title was also used for commanders of cohorts originally raised from Roman citizens, but the latter ranked with prefects of quingenary cohorts for promotion purposes. The level of tribune in a legion or of a milliary cohort was known as the *militia secunda*, the first appointment as *praefectus cohortis* being the *militia prima*. At the second level in the middle of the second century there were 141 posts in the legions, perhaps around thirty – forty in milliary cohorts, so giving a total of around 180 in all, a useful figure to work with. As a result some ninety first *militia* officers might not receive promotion, in which case they would simply hand over to their successors and retire.

So far the equestrian would have been seeking his commissions at the hands of governors, for they had in their gift posts as *praefectus cohortis* and as *tribunus legionis*, both *laticlavius* and *angusticlavius*, with the emperor's consent of course. The aspiring officer would have armed himself with letters of recommendation from influential people, as can be illustrated from Pliny's letters. But the third level, the *militia tertia*, with some ninety posts as *praefectus alae* (the older title is *praefectus equitum*, prefect of cavalry), came directly under the emperor's eye. The man who secured promotion into this grade would usually have to take up his post in a different province from that or those in which his previous posts had been held. Again there would be elimination. There would be no promotion available for some ninety of the men in the *secunda militia*. This meant that perhaps two-thirds of the original 270 had been weeded out, as unsuitable for promotion to the third grade and a cavalry command. This must have been very necessary, for again the men who began their military careers with the command of nearly five hundred men had no preliminary training except as magistrates. Once more the principle was maintained that the leader in peace could lead in war.

From the time of Hadrian there was a fourth level, the *quarta militia*. The commanders of the milliary *alae* which had been created towards the end of the first century A.D. henceforth were to form an elite, perhaps nine men to be selected from the ninety commanders of quingenary *alae*. No province had more than one of these rare units.

Beyond the *militiae* lay the procuratorships, a steadily expanding body of posts reserved for the equestrian order. They included the officials responsible for all accounting in the imperial provinces, in Britain for example, the *procurator provinciae Britanniae*, and the emperor's concerns in the senatorial provinces, the heads of depart-

ial View, Housesteads, looking west along the wall from the fort   *Philipson Studio*

The Rudge Cup. A Roman bronze bowl listing some of the Wall forts.

Sestertius of Hadrian from the River Tyne at Newcastle (enlarged)

Photographs by courtesy of The Museum of Antiquities, University of Newcastle upon Tyn

Model of Benwell Fort by W. Bulmer

Aerial View, Housesteads

Aerial View, Chesterholm

Latrine — Housesteads.

Model of part of a granary by W. Bulmer

14

Above
Bath House
Chesters

Right
Aerial View
Chesters

15

TI CLAVDI	MENANDRI
A FVLVI	IVST
TI IVLI	VRBANI
L PVLLI	DAPHNI
L NONI	VICTORIS
Q LOLLI	FEST
L PVPI	VICTORI

IMP CAESAR DIVI TRAIANI PARTHIC F DIVI NERVAE NEPOS TRA
IANVS HADRIANVS AVG PONT MAX TRIB POT VS COS
NICH TESTAT VI COS III PROCOS
EQVITIB ET PEDITIB QVI MILITAVER IN ALIS DECEM ET TRIB ET COH
TRI TRICIN ALAE EPTEM QVAE APPELLANTVR I PANNONIOR SABINIAN
ET PANNONIOR TAMPIANA ET HISPANOR VETT ER CR ET GALLOR
ET ... ET ... GALLO AF ROSIANA ET VELCONI HIS PANC R ET
NERVIAC GERMAN OPT CEIT IBEROR ET ... RAGETA BORACR ITL
IVRONC ET FIDELVA ... OR OC RETI R EST LAN ... ET I NANGION
... ET IMAIOR SAGITE ET I DELMATAR ... ANTANI EM ... RATA
ET ... ET I SENCRET IM OR INET I MENA ... ET ... NGOR R IGE TA
... DAL ET I BATAVOR ET I NG ROR ET T ... GALLOR ETI
VASCON ... ET II HISP CETIL LON GON ET IASI NE ... DEIN VATAR
... I NERVIOR ET I BRACARACR ET LLINGON

ET I IMI GALLOR ET III BRVCORE ... CVI DE MATERTVS RAETO
ET I GALL ... IN ... OS ET VI THRAC QVAE SVNT IN ILI M
IN VBALA ... MAIOR ET IN POT O QVIN VE ET VIGI ET IN ...
EMERIT I S DIMISS IS HONEST A ... SSION IS ER DONM DEM
IIS Q ... ONEAM QVOR VM NOMINA INA SVB SCRIPTA SVNT ISI V BI
R EMOS T ... ISQEOR VM CINI TATEN DEDIT ET CONNB VM ... O
RIB SVAS ... EN I CHABVISS ENT CVM EST CVM AS ... IS DATA
AVT S IQVI CAELI BESES ENT CVM IIS QVAS POSTE AD VXO
SENT DVM TAXAT SIN GVLIS IN GVLAS A C V I K A ... C
TI IVLIO CANI TONE L V STRASIO R ANNI NO COS
ALAE I PANNONIOR TAM PIANAE CVI PRAEST
FABIVS EX SESQVI PLICARIO SABINVS
G EMELLO B R FI CI PANNON
DESCRIPT IM METRE COGNIT VM ER TAB V L A ENEA QVAE FIXA EST
R OMAE I N M V RO POST T EM PLVM DIVI AVG A D MI NER VAM

ments in Rome and their representatives in provinces or groups of provinces, in such matters as the reassessment of the population for tax purposes (the *census* e.g. *procurator ad census Britanniae*), the recruiting of gladiators (e.g. *procurator familiae gladiatorum per Gallias Bretannias Hispanias Germanias et Raetiam*), the organisation of the imperial post (*praefectus vehiculorum*), and the control of the emperor's personal property (*procurator rationis privatae*), governors of certain provinces without a legionary garrison, prefects of the Italian and provincial fleets e.g. *praefectus classis Britannicae*. Although examples of posts including Britain related to the imperial post and the emperor's personal property are not attested there can be no doubt that such posts existed. All these posts were ranged into categories according to their pay-scale, 60,000 sesterces (*sexagenarius*), 100,000 sesterces (*centenarius*), 200,000 sesterces (*ducenarius*), 300,000 sesterces (*trecenarius*). Beyond them lay the great secretariats in Rome, correspondence (*ab epistulis*), finance (*a rationibus*), petitions (*a libellis*), and others, and the great prefectures, of the fire service (*praefectus vigilum*), corn supply (*praefectus annonae*), of Egypt (*praefectus Aegypti*), and of the guard (*praefectus praetorio*).

The question has been raised to what extent the equestrian military service was genuine, and to what extent it merely provided a route to be covered as quickly as possible to the procuratorships and prefectures. While clearly men had to be found for the latter posts and would be promoted quickly it seems that there were a number of mature and responsible equestrian officers who spent some time in military service. But it will be noted that they had no security of tenure; their length of service depended on the emperor continuing to maintain them in their present post or offering them a further one.

A typical career is that of Maenius Agrippa:

M(arco) Maenio C(ai) f(ilio) Cor(nelia) Agrippae L. Tusidio Campestri, hospiti divi Hadriani, patri senatoris, praef(ecto) coh(ortis) II Fl(aviae) Britton(um) equitat(ae), electo a divo Hadriano et misso in expeditionem Britannicam, trib(uno) coh(ortis) I Hispanor(um) equitat(ae), praef(ecto) alae Gallor(um) et Pannonior(um) catafractatae, proc(uratori) Aug(usti) praef(ecto) classis Britannicae, proc(uratori) provinciae Britanniae, equo publico, patrono municipi.

The inscription, set up under the emperor Antoninus Pius, mentions that Maenius Agrippa had been a personal friend (*hospes*) of Hadrian, now deified (*divi Hadriani*), and that he was the father of a senator (*pater senatoris*), entry into the senate being common in the second generation for equestrian families, particularly distinguished ones. He had begun his military career as prefect of a *cohors equitata* in Moesia inferior (Romania) and had been picked out by Hadrian to go on a British campaign, where he took command as tribune of a milliary *cohors equitata*, *I Hispanorum*, which had recently been doubled in size, at Maryport. A cavalry command as prefect of an *ala*, again in Moesia inferior, followed, and then he entered the procuratorships with the command of the British fleet (100,000 sesterces), based on

Boulogne, and returned to Britain as procurator (accounting official) responsible directly to the emperor (200,000 sesterces). The *equo publico* refers to his equestrian rank. The patronage of this city (*patronus municipi*) was a common recognition of a successful public career; the statue was set up in gratitude for services he had rendered his city in obtaining privileges from the emperor.

The ordinary soldiers of the *auxilia* (*alae, cohortes, numeri*) were originally not Roman citizens by birth (in contrast to the legions, which were recruited in theory only from Roman citizens, though some only received their citizenship at the moment of joining the legion). They received Roman citizenship on discharge, a powerful inducement to join, and the grant included their children. The spread of Roman citizenship throughout the Empire by this and other means tended to blur the rigid division between the two types of unit, citizen and non-citizen, and as the second century went on more and more citizens enlisted in the *auxilia*, perhaps weighing against the lower pay the better prospects for promotion they would gain by entering a unit with a lower level of talent. The grant by the emperor Caracalla of citizenship to all but a few groups in the Empire eliminated the distinction between citizen and non-citizen units and the gap between legions and *auxilia* continued to narrow till cavalry became the decisive arm from at the latest the middle of the third century.

The men of the *auxilia* were recruited from non-citizens, as has been said, though with an increasing proportion of citizens. They tended in the first place, not unnaturally, to be from provinces where there were few citizens, or frontier regions of otherwise civilised provinces, even from outside the Empire altogether. As civilisation and peaceful conditions spread, the best recruiting grounds tended more and more to be the frontier districts. Although the mutinies on the Rhine in A.D. 69-70 dealt a temporary blow to the principle of stationing men close to their homes local recruiting was soon resumed, helped by the tendency to move whole units very rarely after the middle of the second century A.D. It was a volunteer army, and conscription was only resorted to in moments of crisis. Occasionally, however, recalcitrants were forcibly drafted into the *auxilia*.

The man enlisting in the *auxilia* would go through a careful examination of his medical fitness and investigation of his claim to free birth and would also be put through some basic training before being entered on the rolls of his unit. What happened to him after being escorted to his unit will be discussed in the next section. Here his prospects of promotion will be considered.

Cavalry ranked higher and were paid more than infantry in the *auxilia*. To enlist in the *alae* our recruit might have had to pass a height qualification; in the *cohortes equitatae* he would usually start as an infantryman and only after some service be accepted for training as a cavalryman (*eques*). Apart from this basic difference there were two major steps in promotion. The first was to obtain some post or acquire some trade that would render him not liable to fatigues. This

18

right to be immune from fatigues (as an *immunis*) did not carry any extra pay. The second step in promotion was to become a *principalis*, a man with extra pay and responsibilities, either as a junior officer of the century or the *turma*, or on the staff of the commanding officer.

The *auxilia* did not have the large number of different posts and trades that the legion had. They had hospital staff, and the musicians whose main task was to give signals on the march, in camp, and on the battle field, and the clerks of the regiment's orderly room, all among the *immunes*. Above them came the junior officers of the tactical units, the *tesserarius, optio* and *signifer* in the century, the *sesquiplicarius, duplicarius* and *signifer* in the *turma*. The *tesserarius* took his name from the *tessera*, the tablet on which the watch-word was written and which was taken round the guard-posts. His duties are obscure. The *optio*, a post of some antiquity, was the centurion's deputy. The *signifer* was responsible for the *turma's* or century's standard, the *signum*, in battle and for the complicated accounting associated with pay, deductions and savings. The *duplicarius* and *sesquiplicarius* in the *turma* took their names from their pay-grades, twice and one-and-a-half times that of the ordinary cavalryman in this case. Every *principalis* was on one of these two grades, twice and one and a half times the pay of the ordinary soldier in his particular type of unit, and mounted men in the legions and *cohortes equitatae* received more than their infantrymen did. There were two other officers of some importance at century and *turma* level, the *custos armorum*, who was in charge of the armoury, and the *curator*, only found in the *turma*, whose duties are uncertain.

The senior members of the commander's staff ranked equally with the junior officers of the tactical units. The kernel of almost every officer's staff in the Roman army was the *cornicularius*, his adjutant, and the *beneficiarii*, men who were chosen by himself to do whatever duties he assigned to them.

The centurions and decurions of the *auxilia* were for the most part promoted from the ranks of the *auxilia*. Occasionally a legionary ranker was made a centurion or decurion in the *auxilia*, and in provinces where no legions were stationed a man who elsewhere might have sought a direct commission as legionary centurion sought one as decurion of an *ala*. But the vast majority were from the ranks.

SOLDIERS OF THE WALL

I The Forts

These officers and men of the *auxilia* spent their active service in forts. The Roman fort was a development of that most distinctive Roman institution, adopted from other armies and made peculiarly their own, the Roman camp. For centuries Roman armies before settling down for the night had dug a shallow ditch and thrown up a mound with the upcast, in which stakes were fixed. Gaps were left for entrances. More elaborate forms had more and deeper ditches, higher ramparts, protective devices at the entrances. Inside the camp the leather tents of the army on campaign were replaced by timber buildings for longer occupation, particularly in winter. The commander's tent,

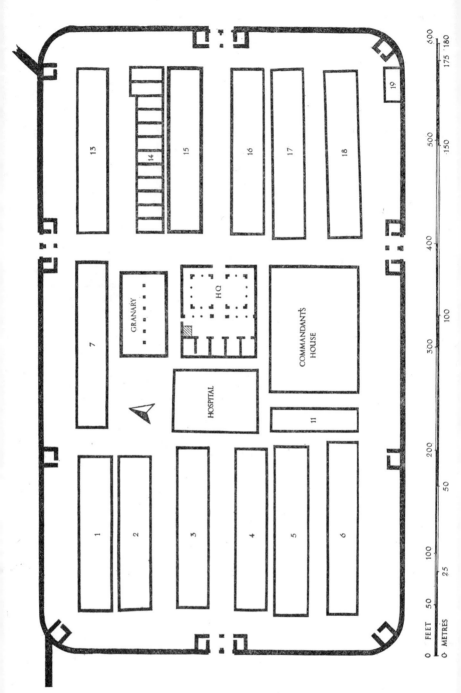

originally both his living quarters and the headquarters, was replaced by a house, and the need for a headquarters was then met by creating a new building. In this was found room for the old tribunal, once a turf platform in the camp where the commanding officer might preside over matters relating to requests or discipline, and for the standards of the unit, once grouped around the tribunal. In the early forts in this country some of these developments are incomplete, but by the late 80's at least the familiar playing card shape was established for the Roman fort (e.g. Fendoch) and in the early second century stone was introduced as a building material. The forts on Hadrian's Wall, which were built in the 120's, had stone walls, and internal buildings with stone or half-timbered walls, but still had an arrangement based on that of the old camp.

The fort was laid out with its front gate (*porta praetoria*) facing the enemy (the north for the forts on the Wall) or the east (as at Housesteads). From it the *via praetoria* ran to the headquarters building, in front of which at right-angles to the *via praetoria* ran the *via principalis*, joining the two main side gates, the *porta principalis sinistra* and *porta principalis dextra*. The part of the fort in front of the *via principalis* was known as the *praetentura:* behind the *principia* was known as the *retentura.* Behind the principal buildings, headquarters, granaries and commander's house ran a minor road, the *via quintana*, which served for loading and unloading outside the granaries. In those forts which projected north of Hadrian's Wall it served the two minor side gates, the *portae quintanae*, which were provided for lateral traffic behind the safety of the Wall. Finally at right angles from the *quintana*, continuing the direction of the *via praetoria*, the *via decumana* led to the rear gate of the fort, the *porta decumana.* Around the fort inside the rampart ran the *intervallum* road, providing more room for sub-units to assemble and allowing free access to the rampart if there was danger.

The central building in the fort was the headquarters building, the *principia.* Several fine examples of this type of building are visible on the Wall and near it (Chesters, Housesteads, Chesterholm, South Shields, a miniature one at Corbridge). It consists essentially of a courtyard surrounded by verandahs, often later converted into little rooms, an aisled cross-hall (*basilica*), in which is the dais (*tribunal*) from which the commanding officer presided over questions of routine and discipline, and a rear range of rooms, normally five in number. The central room, the *aedes*, was reserved for the statue of the emperor and the standards of the unit. The rooms on the tribunal side, the left, were probably for the *cornicularius* and his clerks; those on the other side less certainly were for the *signiferi.* The three central rooms, including the *aedes*, had low stone screens with metal grilles fixed in them, so that the objects of worship in the central shrine could be seen from outside the building, and the clerks could deal with the men without their crossing the threshold of their offices.

On one side of the headquarters building was the commander's house (*praetorium*). This is best seen at Chesters, Housesteads and

CHESTERS FORT

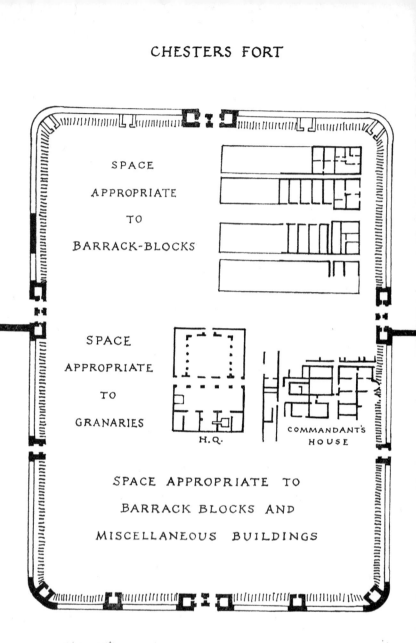

SPACE

APPROPRIATE

TO

BARRACK-BLOCKS

SPACE

APPROPRIATE

TO

GRANARIES

H.Q.

COMMANDANT'S
HOUSE

SPACE APPROPRIATE TO

BARRACK BLOCKS AND

MISCELLANEOUS BUILDINGS

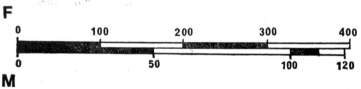

F

| 0 | 100 | 200 | 300 | 400 |

| 0 | | 50 | | 100 | 120 |

M

Corbridge. It normally took the form of a large courtyard house, the equivalent of a large town house or a villa, where the commander, his family and slave household would be accommodated with ease. A bath-suite would normally be attached.

On the other side would be the granaries (*horrea*). These are generally thought to have held one year's supplies; this would clearly be the most convenient arrangement as far as grain was concerned. It is not improbable that an arrangement of bins with a central corridor was used. The visible characteristics of the granary are its raised floor, on dwarf walls (Corbridge) or pillars (Housesteads), ventilation channels below the floor, and buttresses. It has been suggested recently that the buttresses were to take the thrust of the roof, the walls not being completed in stone but with timber louvres to allow the ventilation of the interior of the granary.

A hospital was provided at milliary infantry and at cavalry forts, perhaps at all forts. The Housesteads hospital is in process of being uncovered for display. The normal arrangement seems to have been a number of wards around a central corridor, with a reception area and operating theatre.

There are often other buildings, of uncertain purpose, in the central third of the fort. It would be idle to pretend that all buildings are readily identifiable. The other two-thirds of the fort were taken up with barracks and stables. Little is known of the latter, and the point should be made that even an infantry unit would require accommodation for its carts and draught animals.

The barrack building is directly descended from the tented camp. Originally eight leather tents, each holding eight men, with a larger tent at the end for the centurion, formed the century's accommodation. This is said to have accommodated ten *contubernia*, tent-groups, as two groups of eight would be on duty at any given time in ca p. In front of the tents was space for equipment and the mules that carried the heavy baggage, and another row of tents opposite accommodated the sister-century of the maniple, the two century unit used in the Republic.

When this was rendered in timber or stone it took the form of an L-shaped building, the centurion's quarters being the base of the L, with ten rooms for the men divided by a partition length-wise, so that each *contubernium* of eight men had a space of approximately 270 square feet, which included an inner room where they slept, and an outer room, presumably for equipment. A verandah ran the length of the building, often facing another barrack's verandah with a drain running through the centre between the two buildings. The space allocated to each man varied, cavalry doing better than infantry. Barracks of this type may best be seen at Chesters, those at Housesteads and Greatchesters being of a later, fourth century type, discussed below (p. 41).

There was no central cookhouse, cooking being done in ovens set in the rampart back or on the ground floor of towers (Birdoswald has good examples). The method was simple: a fire was lit in the oven

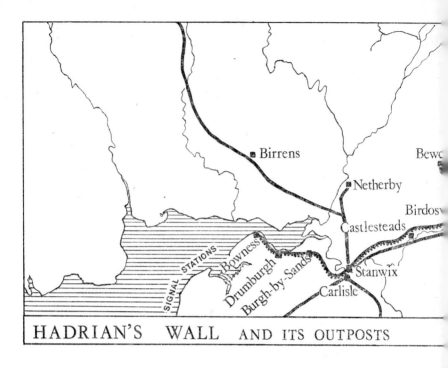

HADRIAN'S WALL AND ITS OUTPOSTS

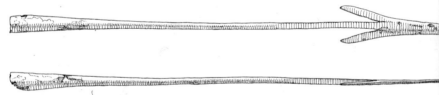

Above
Barbed iron spearhead, found in a well in the fort at Carvoran

Far right
Iron arrowhead with part of the wooden shaft, from Housesteads
4th century

Right
Barbed iron spearhead, found with a coin of Constantius I at
Housesteads

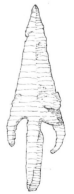

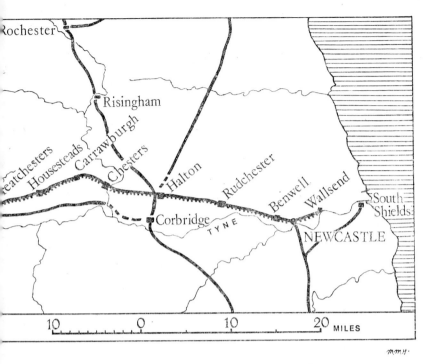

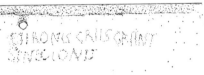

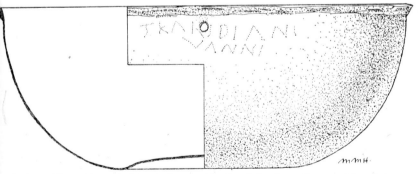

Brass cauldron with punched inscriptions marking it as belonging to Vannus of the cavalry troop (t(urma)) commanded by Kandianus and, at some other time, to Crescentinus of the troop commanded by Tiro, and later to Senecio. From Prestwick Carr, Northumberland. 2nd century

itself, the ashes raked out, and the bread or whatever was being cooked was put in. The ovens were of stone with clay tops which had to be constantly renewed. The soldiers may also have used open hearths. Where exactly they ate their food is uncertain.

Also in the rampart back were the latrines. As in the provision of water supply and drainage and in the hospital care, the Roman army here surpassed all but modern armies in their standard of care for hygiene. The Housesteads latrine illustrates clearly the care for constantly flowing water through a large drain over which seating was arranged. There was even a channel for the soldiers to wash the sponges they used instead of toilet paper, and stone lavers in which apparently the hands could be washed.

Water supply to the fort was taken care of by aqueducts (Corbridge, Greatchesters, and Lanchester have fine visible remains). Housesteads appears to have no supply to the fort itself, though the Knag Burn was available close at hand, and the fort bath-house, a great consumer of water, stood close to it. At Housesteads in particular there has been considerable care taken to catch and store rainwater in tanks – some visitors have felt that this would in itself provide an ample supply! There is also evidence at all forts for the provision of drains to cope with rainwater and drainage from buildings. The elaborate system of channels at Housesteads to run off water from the tanks into the latrine well repays detailed examination.

One major building of importance to the life of the unit was placed outside the fort, the bath-house. The original fort plan had developed from the camp, with no provision for this building, which would have taken up a lot of space in the fort, and represented a considerable fire risk. The bath-houses of Hadrian's Wall, in so far as they have been explored, show a standard plan. The bather entered successively warmer steam filled rooms (*tepidaria*) till the hottest room of all was reached (*calidarium*). He might on the way have rubbed himself with oil. In the hot room a small hot bath was available if desired. From the *calidarium* the bather returned through the warm rooms to the cold room (*frigidarium*), where he splashed himself with cold water to close up the pores, possibly aiding the process by making use of a cold water bath. An alternative form of cleaning provided was the sweating-room (*sudatorium*) where dry heat only was employed. The finest example of a military bath-house exposed on the line of the Wall is that at Chesters, although it is perhaps made confusing for the visitor by later modifications.

A feature which probably existed outside most if not all forts was the parade-ground, required not only for parades but also for drill, weapon training and the religious ceremonies to be performed by units of the army on important dates in the official military calendar of religious festivals. There is no certain example on the Wall itself though there is evidence for one at South Shields. The best known perhaps is that at Hardknott.

There is one more building of an official character, but of importance

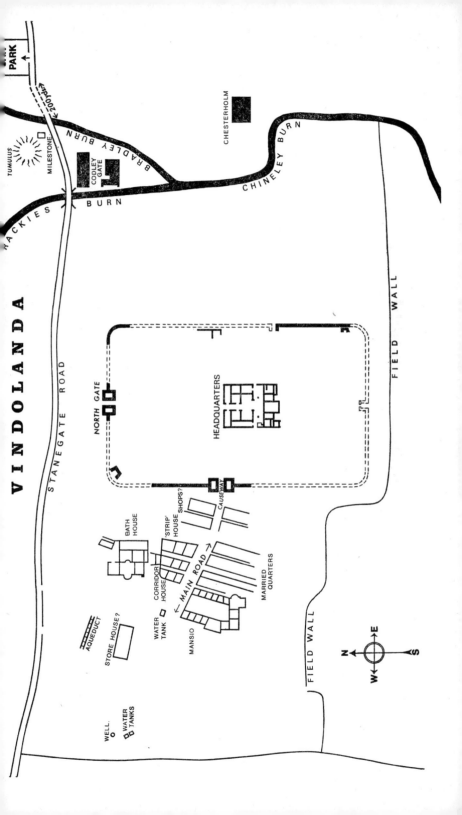

for administration rather than for the army, the *mansio*. This was a large building, generally resembling a more elaborate version of a commander's house, providing accommodation for the night for messengers of the imperial post and other official travellers. The finest example on the Wall is that newly exposed and identified at Chesterholm. Such buildings are known also at Benwell and Corbridge.

There were no temples inside the forts, and no provision for worship apart from the official worship of the gods who watched over Rome, including the deified emperors, associated with the *aedes* in the headquarters building and also with the parade-ground, as the fine series of altars from Maryport and Birdoswald show. Otherwise religion was a private concern, and the second century temples at Housesteads were kept not merely outside the fort but outside the vallum, like all civilian activity. Later the temples were closer to the forts, as at Carrawburgh, where the arrangement is particularly interesting. The ancient shrine of Coventina (the stone structure is Roman but the spring worship is likely to be far older) is not far from the later Mithraeum with the Nymphaeum in its turn very close to the Mithraeum, though only the side of its tank is visible above the turf today. The Corbridge temples form another interesting group.

The bath-house, *mansio* and the temples were the most prominent buildings in the *vicus*, the village which grew up outside almost every Roman fort. The elements in this growth varied, but the basic attraction was a large number of men with more ready money paid regularly than the district was likely to see from all its other resources put together. There would be drinking houses, brothels, shops. Wives and families of the soldiers, official or unofficial, swelled the numbers of residents and consumers. Dr. St. Joseph's aerial photographs show clearly the size of the settlement that extended all round three sides of Housesteads, and the visible remains there and the information now available about the *vicus* at Chesterholm show that these settlements were of considerable importance and must have had a marked effect on the economy of the surrounding district. The next stage, not to be explored here, was the garrison towns of Carlisle and Corbridge.

From this brief survey of the buildings we turn to consider the lives of the people living in them.

II The Soldiers

Little more needs to be said of the commanding officer. Isolated from his men and even from his officers by the gap in social rank, he lived the life of a country gentleman in his house with his family and slave household around him. Apart from the routine of hearing requests, exercising his disciplinary powers and signing documents, in peacetime conditions, which was the norm on the Wall, he need do little else unless he was keen enough to supervise an intensive training programme. Hunting was one of the few diversions open to him.

The men in all but specialised units such as the archers from the Middle East (for example the Hamians at Carvoran) were locally recruited volunteers. They exchanged the relative uncertainty and

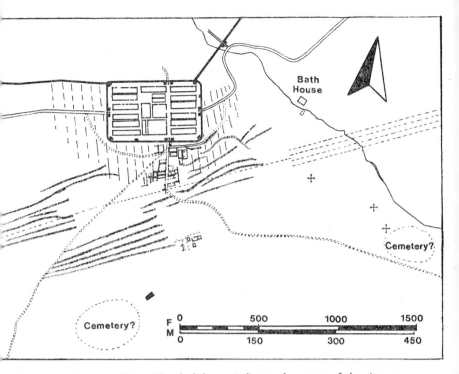

Housesteads Fort and Vicus. The shaded area indicates the extent of the vicus as revealed by aerial photography, the crosses indicate the findspots of religious inscriptions and sculptures. (Based on E. Birley, Research on Hadrian's Wall, Fig. 25)

hardship of subsistence farming for regular pay, twenty-five years of being looked after and provided with food, clothing and accommodation, and retirement with the status of a Roman citizen. After acceptance and initial training they would be delivered to their unit. There their life would centre around the barrack room, particularly the *contubernium*, their own little section of eight men. They in theory would be kept in training by regular exercises, though as has been already hinted this would depend very much on the conscientiousness of the commanding officer. In addition to this reinforcement of the basic skills of marching, riding, manoeuvring, camp building, weapon training, and swimming there were the fatigues which those who had not yet become *immunes* would have to share: guards at the headquarters and the gates, prowler patrols, bath-house and latrine fatigues, batman duty for the junior officers. All these were carefully recorded, as we know from surviving documents, to ensure an equitable distribution of duties. The Roman army had no weekends, although there may have been some compensation in the numerous festivals of the official military religious calendar, if these were observed as holidays. Leave (*commeatus*) was granted but on what basis is not known.

No doubt the odd spell of duty outside the fort was appreciated, and although the emperor Trajan objected to the practice it is clear that for one reason or another units had a fair number of men out of camp. Escort duties, collection of clothing and provisions, horses perhaps, draught animals, all might call men away from camp, apart from the fatigue parties collecting fuel. It may be that from the Wall forts men went to do a turn of duty in the turrets and milecastles. All these absences were carefully noted and a check kept on the number in camp and out. To the duty rosters already mentioned can be added a daily report containing the names of the men on guard at the head-quarters, the watchword for the day, and the numbers of men leaving or returning to camp. Men absent from camp had individual records noting when they left and why, and when they returned. Each year a full return of the unit's strength, with accessions and losses, temporary and permanent, during the year, was sent in to the governor, for eventual transmission to Rome.

There were a number of possible variations on daily routine to brighten up life apart from being sent off on a duty outside camp. The special ceremonies connected with the army's religious year have already been referred to. In January the oath of allegiance to the emperor was renewed, and the year then went its way with commemoration of the birthdays and accession days of deified emperors, the traditional festivals of Rome, like the Saturnalia on December 25th, and the special rites connected with the standards, symbols of loyalty to the unit. The one common point to these men was that they belonged to and served Rome, and shared her traditions and her emperor. If the commanding officer kept a proper field training programme going, there would be route marches, living under canvas (leather actually) construction of camps and entrenchments, mock warfare, etc. Such manoeuvres on rare occasions might have to be carried out under the eye of the emperor himself. We have fragments of speeches made by Hadrian to the Army of Africa after such a review.

One other element in the soldier's official life was the pay parade, not a weekly event but every quarter. These were ceremonial occasions as well as of considerable utilitarian value, and we have a description of the associated parade. The documents relating to pay are concerned not so much with what the soldier received over the counter, or rather between the grille and the stone screen in the headquarters building, but with the various compulsory deductions from pay, for clothing, food, weapons, and bedding (straw). The *signifer* recorded the fixed amount which was deducted to cover these items each quarter, and the actual amounts charged against this. A credit or debit balance was carried forward.

The soldier might also save out of his pay, depositing the money with the *signifer*, and withdrawing it on demand. The legionaries had half of their donatives, gifts from the emperor on special occasions to citizen troops, saved compulsorily for them against the day of retirement. It is not clear if the auxiliaries also benefited from donatives, but it is difficult to see how they could have been long excluded, as

30

their importance grew and the distinction between citizen and non-citizen troops became less meaningful.

It is difficult to say how much free time the soldier had. There are two opposing influences, the desire in any army to keep the troops occupied, against the dangers of boredom and discontent, and the natural slackness of peace-time conditions. Much free time must have been spent in the *vicus*, where so many people were anxious for a share in the money in the soldier's arm-purse. Here would be the soldier's family.

The Roman soldier till the early third century could not contract a marriage recognised in Roman law while serving. This did not inhibit the soldiers, with twenty-five years to serve, from entering into unions which were no doubt celebrated after the forms of local custom, and treated as marriages by all concerned. The state took no cognizance of them till the moment of discharge.

Discharge requires our special attention, for the privileges gained on discharge were among the main attractions to service in the *auxilia*. The soldier on discharge was entitled to receive a copy of a decree posted in Rome which recited the units discharging men in that year and the names of the men discharged. In the time of Hadrian it granted to these men, on being given an honourable discharge, Roman citizenship. It extended the citizenship also to their children, including those already born during service, and their descendants. The soldiers also were granted full recognition of their marriage in Roman law (*conubium*) with the wives they had at the time of the grant or of a future marriage if they were bachelors. The wives were not granted the citizenship themselves, but their existence and that of their children is assumed by this official document.

The regular granting of the citizenship to time-expired auxiliaries seems to have begun with the emperor Claudius. Under Antoninus Pius a limitation of the privilege of citizenship to the soldier and children born to him after discharge was introduced, possibly to stimulate the children born during their father's service to enlist as the quickest way of obtaining the citizenship denied to them. The edict of Caracalla bestowing citizenship on all but a few groups in the empire made the diploma unnecessary, his father Severus apparently having already conceded the right of soldiers to marry during service. In the fourth century there is a reference to the transport of the wives and families of a transferred unit, but it will be recalled that most of the units on the Wall itself did not change stations after the beginning of the third century A.D. In such circumstances it seems likely that birth in the village outside the fort and growing up there, service in the fort with a family in the village, retirement to the village, was the natural life cycle. In the late empire, from the early fourth century, occupations of importance to the State, above all that of soldier, became compulsorily hereditary, but at all times there seems to have been a tendency for father to be followed by sons into the army.

It was no certain thing that a man would survive till retirement. Of 100 men enlisted in Africa at about twenty only half would be alive at the age of forty-four, according to the most important study of life expectation in the Roman Empire. To console the soldier was the fact that civilians had a lower expectation of life to this point, though they did better later on, suggesting that the soldier without the special care lavished on his health by the army proved vulnerable to civilian diseases. He could make his will, orally if need be, so that if he wished what he had could be left to his unofficial wife and children, and records survive of the accounting by the army to the heir for the deceased's assets. In retirement the auxiliary veteran would have the dignity of citizenship, and the special privileges of veterans in regard to certain forms of taxation and civic duties. For money he would have to rely on his own savings, though it is possible he may also have had some money from donatives from the emperor. At the age of forty-five it would not be impossible for him to enter an occupation or trade or take up farming.

The soldier on death might be cremated or, from the beginning of the third century, inhumed. Both practices continued side by side in the third century, but after the late third century cremation tended to disappear. Ashes would be put into a container (urns, *amphorae*, glass jars, lead canisters, stone coffins and tiled tombs are all attested); bodies buried in a coffin, normally wooden, though stone, brick, tile or lead might also be used. In either case the remains would be laid to rest in a cemetery away from the fort; burials in an inhabited area were not allowed. We know little of the cemeteries of the forts on the Wall apart from a few locations. The carrying out of the funeral arrangements, sometimes laid down by the dead man himself, would be a private matter for the dead man's heir or heirs, who might also put up a tombstone. In the legions there are traces of special arrangements for ensuring decent burial, either by deductions from pay or later by forming little clubs of junior officers of the same rank who paid subscriptions, but there is no evidence as yet for special arrangements in the *auxilia*.

What religious beliefs would the soldier hold? He was expected of course to take part in the observation of the military religious calendar. Only to the Christian or the Jew would this cause difficulties. Others would recognise a religious duty to pray for the welfare of the emperor and the empire, be prepared to honour the gods of Rome as their own gods under a different name, and respect the god-emperors. It was a test of political loyalty, not of religious belief. Otherwise the soldier was free to choose from a bewildering variety of gods, which may be categorised as the ancient gods of Greece and Rome, the native gods, the gods brought in by units from their original recruiting ground overseas, or by other means e.g. by traders, or the religions which for one reason or another managed to become more than purely local in appeal. A number of factors prevented this variety from producing utter confusion. Gods originally worshipped elsewhere might be identified with local gods as corresponding in their general attributes and sphere of influence, e.g. war, love, trade, hunting, etc. There was no tendency to despise local gods; on the contrary, the

SCENE FROM TRAJAN'S COLUMN

*Regular auxiliary cavalry in action. Note the mail shirts, over short-sleeved tunics,
leather breeches, swords and oval shields.*

SCENE FROM TRAJAN'S COLUMN

Regular auxiliary infantry standing on a temporary wooden bridge. The soldiers held spears in their right hands (originally metal, now missing).

SCENE FROM TRAJAN'S COLUMN

Sarmatian cavalry with characteristic scale armour, here seen fighting the Romans; later employed as troops by the Roman Army.

SCENE FROM TRAJAN'S COLUMN

Moorish horsemen; these are irregular units, following their own native practice in riding and fighting, in contrast with the regular auxiliary cavalry. Note their native costume, characteristic hairstyle and use of rope for reins.

36

SCENE FROM TRAJAN'S COLUMN

Auxiliary archer in characteristic Eastern costume on left; an auxiliary soldier in standard uniform guards a camp while legionaries build and forage.

SCENE FROM TRAJAN'S COLUMN

The suovetaurilia, the emperor sacrifices a pig, sheep and bull on behalf of the army.

Left

Mars, the god of war, on a
Roman sword found at
South Shields.

Below

An enamelled belt mounting
from South Shields.

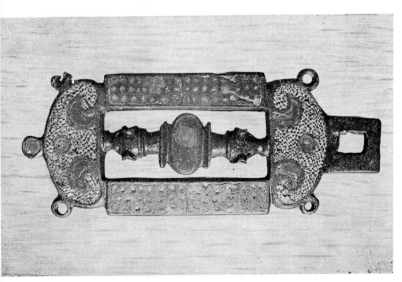

Above. Temple of Antenociticus, Ber

*Left. Head of Antenociticus from his
shrine at Benwell*

soldiers were keenly conscious of the invisible presence of spirits presiding over woods, streams, and other localities, and officers and soldiers from elsewhere in the empire freely offered to purely local deities. Worship of even the most outlandish gods was frequently linked with emperor-worship, dedications to the *numen Augusti,* and worship of the spirits presiding over the various units and even individual buildings. There was no intolerance, except of religions which were suspect because of inhuman practices (Druidism) or of secret abominable rites coupled with apparent atheism (Christianity).

It is not possible here to discuss further the enormous subject of Roman religion. Mithraism, which has been treated separately in a useful publication of the Newcastle Museum of Antiquities, is important among other things in that it shows the defects of the other forms of religion available which it sought to supply. Such defects were their lack of a close personal relationship with the god, of the promise of ever-increasing knowledge of him, of a satisfying glimpse of immortality, and of a strong ethical code. Christianity was to supply all these needs, but it was slow to penetrate the army, and the evidence for it on the Wall, even in the fourth century, when it became legal and enjoyed imperial favour, is slight.

EPILOGUE – THE LATTER DAYS ON THE WALL

As has been said earlier, the materials are simply not available to write an account of the way in which changes in the structure of army and administration affected Roman Britain and the Wall in particular. Even in the period up to the middle of the third century importan. changes were taking place which cannot be adequately chronicledt The full nature of Septimius Severus's changes implied in the grant of the right to marry is not known; the possibility of married quarters outside the forts can only be aired. The names of the units on the Wall do not change; their organisation must have done.

Looking at the evidence from excavation for changes in building inside the forts, the points that may be noted are as follows. The evidence from Housesteads, visible there, that an ordinary barrack block at the beginning of the fourth century was being rebuilt as six separate units, with corroborative evidence from Greatchesters and High Rochester, suggests that the living accommodation was being designed to make provision for fewer men in more comfortable conditions. In headquarters buildings there is apparently a move to provide living accommodation attached to the offices at the rear of the building e.g. at Chesterholm and at Corbridge. That is all that can be said in the present state of knowledge, for in fact very little work has been done inside forts on the Wall in this century. It should be emphasised that there is clearly a considerable degree of continuity, in the basic lay-out of buildings at least.

There have been various attempts to suggest that in the last days the Wall was garrisoned by a peasant militia, and that they moved their families into the forts, which became fortified villages, and abandoned the *vici.* The evidence for this is far from conclusive, and recent work at Chesterholm has shown a *vicus* in occupation after 369, the beginning of the last period on the Wall in the conventional and still useful sub-divisions. What evidence there is, from the *Notitia Dignitatum*, from the lay-out of the forts, and from the fact that the Picts never settled permanently south of the Forth-Clyde line, suggests that the Wall was held by recognisable units of the Roman Army right up to the end of Roman Britain, which may be taken here as the apparently final loss of contact with the central administration in Rome in 410 A.D. What happened thereafter is an almost unexplored problem, which cannot be entered into here.

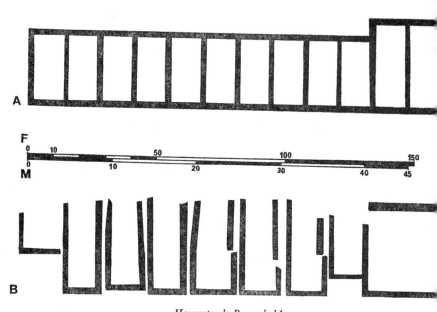

Housesteads Barrack 14.
(A) Second century plan.   (B) As rebuilt in the fourth century.   (Based on Wilkes).

THE REGIMENTS OF THE WALL

The evidence for the units that were stationed in the Wall forts, including the outpost forts and the four Cumberland Coast forts which formed part of the Hadrianic frontier complex comes from inscriptions that allow us to deduce that the unit referred to was in garrison. Often there is an element of doubt; a unit may build a fort, members of it may make a dedication, but the unit may not be in garrison. Diplomas, the copies of grants of privilege on discharge referred to above (p. 31), give lists of units and are dated, so they at least demonstrate the presence of a unit in Britain at a given date; the *Notitia Dignitatum*, dated to the early fifth century, shows the units then in garrison at named forts, some of which can be identified. Many units first attested in Wall forts in the early third century were still in the same forts at the time of the *Notitia;* the *Notitia* list appears at the end of this chapter.

Of the over seventy attested *alae* and *cohortes* which served in Britain thirty-seven are known to have served in these forts. This proportion may seem to be high, but it must be remembered that there is a greater amount of preserved evidence from the Wall area than elsewhere in the province. The regiments that served on the Wall were recruited originally from the normal recruiting grounds: Gaul (Gallorum, Aquitanorum, Lingonum, Nerviorum) eleven; Germany inside the Empire (Germanorum, Baetasiorum, Batavorum, Cugernorum, Frisiavonum, Tungrorum, Vangionum) eight; Spain (Hispanorum, Asturum, Vardullorum) six; the Balkans (Dacorum, Delmatarum, Pannoniorum, Thracum) eight and Switzerland (Raetorum) one. Only one unit, the Hamii, were specialists, archers from the Middle East (Syria); only one was raised in Britain itself (Cornovii, from the Welsh border country). All but the Hamians would be kept up to strength by recruiting from the province where they were stationed, Britain, so their names reflect their origins, not their 'nationality' when in Britain.

alae   Of the fifteen cavalry regiments securely attested in Britain only four are certainly associated with the Wall at any time. Such units if on the Wall were best placed close to the main routes north, and it is there that we find them in the early third century. Pride of place must go to the:

ala Augusta Gallorum Petriana milliaria civium Romanorum   This was the biggest cavalry unit in Britain, the province's only *ala milliaria*. Named almost certainly after a former famous commander, T. Pomponius Petra, it was involved in the civil wars of 69-70 as part of the army in Germany before it appeared in Britain, where it is first attested in the diploma for 98. At that time it does not appear to have been of milliary size, a size first attested in the diploma for 122. At a time earlier than 98 it had been stationed at Corbridge, as the fine tombstone now in Hexham Priory shows. By 98 it had won the honorary titles *civium Romanorum,* a block grant of citizenship to the men serving in the unit at the time as a reward of valour. The award was added to the unit's titles, though future recruits would remain noncitizens till discharge in the normal way.

When precisely the unit came to Stanwix on the Wall is uncertain, as are its movements during the second century. It was at Stanwix at the time of the *Notitia*.

alae quingenariae
ala I Hispanorum Asturum   The Astures were a hill-folk of north-west Spain who provided Britain with at least two cavalry and two infantry regiments. This unit was in Britain in 98, is attested at Benwell at the beginning of the third century, and was still there at the time of the *Notitia*.

ala II Asturum   Attested in Britain in 122, this unit was at Chesters from the time of Ulpius Marcellus, more likely to be the well-known governor of the 180's than the hypothetical governor of that name in the early third century. At Chesters it stayed, and is recorded there in the *Notitia*.

ala I Pannoniorum Sabiniana   First attested in Britain in 122, it may have been at South Shields for a time in the second century, but in the *Notitia* it appears at Halton. It was raised originally in Pannonia (Hungary).

cohortes milliariae   There are only seven of these large units attested in Britain, and they appear to have been concentrated in the Wall area, compensating for the absence of the relatively distant legions.

I Aelia Dacorum   Attested in Britain in 146, this unit is well represented by inscriptions at Birdoswald, where it is first attested in the early third century, and where it appears in the *Notitia*. A lost inscription may show it at Bewcastle under Hadrian. It was raised originally in Dacia (Rumania).

I Nervana Germanorum equitata   Five of the seven milliary cohorts known in Britain were *equitata*, a sign of the usefulness of this type of unit. This unit was in Britain by 122. There are inscriptions of it from Burgh-by-Sands and from Birrens. An inscription at Netherby dedicated to Cocidius may belong to Bewcastle, where the god's shrine was, and is not necessarily evidence for it in garrison at Netherby.

I Aelia Hispanorum equitata   After garrisoning Ardoch in the first century as a quingenary cohort it came to Maryport, where under Hadrian it was doubled in size. It was certainly at Netherby in the third century, but in the *Notitia* it appears at Axelodunum (Castlesteads) at a time when apparently Netherby had been given up.

I Tungrorum   These two regiments of Tungrians were raised originally in Germania inferior, in the area of modern Belgium. The two cohorts may have been among those at the victory of Mons Graupius under Agricola, though there is no proof that they were already milliary. This cohort was milliary by 103, but in 122 and for some years afterwards it was at half-strength as a detachment was posted to Noricum (modern Austria). It may have been at Birdoswald under Hadrian. The unit appears at Castlecary building at full strength under the emperor Antoninus Pius, but it was not necessarily in garrison there. An inscription from Cramond is less easily dated. It is well attested at Housesteads in the third century and is located there in the *Notitia*. As in the case of its sister cohort, though a milliary cohort its commander was called prefect.

II Tungrorum equitata   This cohort also had a detachment on service elsewhere, in Raetia (Eining, Bavaria), attested there in 147 and 153. It was at Birrens in 158. Inscriptions from Castlesteads show the unit there in 241, but it had been replaced there by *I Aelia Hispanorum equitata* by the time of the *Notitia*.

I Vangionum equitata   In Britain as early as 103, it has left inscriptions at Benwell; the daughter of a commander was buried at Chesters. It was at Risingham at the beginning of the third century, where it is well attested. The unit was originally raised in Germania superior (the middle and upper Rhineland).

I fida Vardullorum equitata   In Britain in 98, neither then nor in 105 is it shown as milliary, but appears as such in 122. At Lanchester 175-76, and making a dedication at Castlecary at some time in the second century, it appears at High Rochester in the early third century. It was raised originally in north-west Spain.

cohortes quingenariae   It is perhaps hardly surprising that of the almost fifty quingenary cohorts attested in Britain about half at one time or another found themselves on the Wall, in contrast with the cavalry regiments, few of which are attested on the Wall. Just over thirty were *equitatae*, and again about half had Wall associations.

I Aquitanorum equitata   First attested in Britain in 122, it has left an inscription at Carrawburgh which may be Hadrianic, but was building at Brough-on-Noe under the governor Iulius Verus in the 150's. This unit was originally raised in south-west France.

II Asturum equitata   First attested in Britain in 105. The unit was at Greatchesters in the third century. The *Notitia* gives the garrison as *I Asturum*, but it seems more likely that this is an error for *II* than that *II Asturum* had been replaced by *I Asturum*.

I Baetasiorum civium Romanorum   First attested in Britain in 103, it was at Bar Hill, probably during the first period of occupation of the Antonine Wall, at Maryport, presumably during the period of return to Hadrian's Wall, at Old Kilpatrick during the second period on the Antonine Wall, and had moved to Reculver by the time of the *Notitia*. It may indeed have been at Reculver from the early third century. It was originally raised in Germania inferior, in the area of modern Holland.

I Batavorum equitata   In Britain by 122, it has left building inscriptions at Carvoran, which may in fact have come from the vallum, and at Castlesteads, where it may have been in garrison. The unit is well attested at Carrawburgh, where it was certainly from the time of Severus or Caracalla, and where it was at the time of the *Notitia*. It was originally raised in Germania inferior, in the area of modern Holland.

I Aelia Classica   In Britain in 146, it appears in the *Notitia* as stationed at Tunnocelum, tentatively identified as Moresby, on the Cumberland coast.

I Cornoviorum   Only attested by the *Notitia*, stationed at Newcastle. It is the only unit known on the Wall which was apparently originally raised in Britain.

I Ulpia Traiana Cugernorum civium Romanorum   The titles of Ulpia Traiana (Trajan's Own might be an acceptable rendering) were gained between the diplomas of 103 and 122, as was the honorary title of Roman citizens. An altar at Carrawburgh might indicate that the unit was at some time in garrison there. The unit was originally raised in Germania inferior, in the area of modern Holland.

I Delmatarum equitata   In Britain by 122, it was at Maryport under the emperor Antoninus Pius, later at Chesters, and perhaps at High Rochester. The unit was originally raised in Dalmatia (modern Yugoslavia).

II Delmatarum equitata It was in Britain by 105. There is an inscription, probably of the third century, from Carvoran, and it appears there in the *Notitia*.

I Frisiavonum It was in Britain by 105. It appears at Rudchester in the *Notitia*. An altar at Carrawburgh need only be a personal expression of piety to Coventina. Frisia is in modern Holland.

IV Gallorum equitata It was in Britain by 122. It is attested at a number of forts, including Castlesteads, Risingham and Castle Hill, on the Antonine Wall. It was at Chesterholm under the emperor Caracalla and was still there at the time of the *Notitia*.

V Gallorum equitata In Britain by 122, by 222 it was the garrison at South Shields, but by the time of the *Notitia* it had been replaced by the *numerus barcariorum Tigrisiensium*. There is an inscription of this unit from Cramond also.

I Hamiorum sagittariorum This specialist regiment was in Britain by 122. It was stationed at Carvoran at the end of the reign of Hadrian and again under the emperor Marcus Aurelius in the 160's, and it seems probable as has been suggested recently that it remained at the fort throughout the first period of occupation of the Antonine Wall. It was at Bar Hill on the Antonine Wall in the second period of occupation of that wall, the Baetasians having been there during the first.

I Hispanorum equitata See above under the milliary cohorts.

I Lingonum equitata In Britain by 105, at High Rochester under the governor Lollius Urbicus in the early 140's, it was at Lanchester in the period 238-44.

II Lingonum equitata In Britain by 98, at Ilkley under Marcus and Verus in the 160's, and also at some time at Moresby. In the *Notitia* it appears at Congavata, identified as Drumburgh.

IV Lingonum equitata In Britain by 103, its only known place of garrison is Wallsend, where inscriptions attest it, probably all of the third century, and where it is placed by the *Notitia*. All these three regiments were originally raised in Germania superior, in the area of eastern France.

II Nerviorum civium Romanorum This unit was in Britain by 98. Inscriptions come from Wallsend, Carrawburgh (a detachment) and Whitley Castle (213). An inscription near Chesterholm need not imply that the unit was in garrison there. This regiment and the next were raised in Gallia Belgica (modern Belgium).

VI Nerviorum In Britain by 122. It served at Rough Castle under the emperor Antoninus Pius, at Bainbridge in 205 and at an uncertain date at Greatchesters.

I Pannoniorum equitata An inscription from milecastle 42, if originally from Greatchesters, does not necessarily imply that this unit was in garrison there. It was raised originally in Pannonia (modern Hungary).

II Pannoniorum equitata   Attested in Britain in 105. There is a fragmentary inscription of a commander from Beckfoot.

VI Raetorum   The unit is attested at Greatchesters under the emperors Marcus and Verus in the 160's. Raetia covered parts of Switzerland and Germany.

I Thracum equitata civium Romanorum   This regiment was helping with building at Birdoswald in the early third century. It is apparently distinct from the *I Thracum equitata* attested on the 122 diploma and known to be at Bowes in the early third century. Thrace is divided today between southern Bulgaria and Turkey-in-Europe.

II Thracum equitata   In Britain by 103, attested at Mumrills, and at Moresby not earlier than the late second century. In the *Notitia* it is located at Gabrosentum, generally identified as Burrow Walls.

numeri

numerus barcariorum Tigrisiensium   At South Shields in the *Notitia*, not necessarily the same unit as the *numerus barcariorum* attested at Lancaster.

numerus exploratorum Bremeniensium   This unit attested at High Rochester, and the ones that follow seem to belong to a number of extra units attached to Wall and outpost forts in the third century, which supplemented the regular garrisons. They could not have been accommodated in the forts but presumably bivouacked elsewhere, and were probably intended to patrol intensively the area north of the Wall. This unit is attested in the period 238-44.

numerus exploratorum Habitancensium   This unit is attested in 213 at Risingham.

cuneus Frisionum Aballavensium   This unit, of a type formed in the third century, is attested at Papcastle in 241. Its name seems to imply that it had previously garrisoned Burgh-by-Sands (Aballava). The unit was presumably first raised in Frisia (modern Holland).

cuneus Frisiorum Ver.   This unit is attached to Housesteads, Ver. presumably being an abbreviation of a name formed from the fort's name of Vercovicium. The inscription is dated 222-35.

numerus Hnaudifridi   Also based on Housesteads in the third century, clearly originally raised in Germany, taking its name from its present commander or possibly from its original or a former famous commander.

numerus Maurorum Aurelianorum   An inscription from Beaumont shows that this unit was already at Burgh-by-Sands in the middle of the third century, and therefore that its title shows that it had been raised by the emperor Marcus Aurelius in the second. It is at Burgh in the *Notitia*. The Moors came from North Africa.

vexillatio gaesatorum Raetorum   At Greatchesters in the third century, also as an additional unit to the garrisoning cohort.

Raeti gaesati   At Risingham in 213 along with the unit in garrison and the *numerus exploratorum*. It may or may not have been the same unit as the *vexillatio gaesatorum Raetorum*.

sub dispositione viri spectabilis ducis Britanniarum:
(under the control of the Duke of the Britains)

praefectus numeri barcariorum Tigrisiensium Arbeia (South Shields)

N.B. South Shields is in a separate section from the Wall forts, a section which includes the hinterland forts, and which shows signs of considerable reorganisation in the late third century.

item, per lineam valli (further, along the line of the Wall):

tribunus cohortis quartae Lingonum, Segeduno (Wallsend)

tribunus cohortis primae Cornoviorum, Ponte Aelio (Newcastle)

praefectus alae primae Asturum, Conderco (Benwell)

tribunus cohortis primae Frixagorum, Vindobala (Rudchester)

praefectus alae Sabinianae, Hunno (Halton)

praefectus alae secundae Asturum, Cilurno (Chesters)

tribunus cohortis primae Batavorum, Procolitia (Carrawburgh)

tribunus cohortis primae Tungrorum, Borcovicio (Housesteads)

tribunus cohortis quartae Gallorum, Vindolana (Chesterholm)

tribunus cohortis primae Asturum, Aesica (Greatchesters)

tribunus cohortis secundae Dalmatarum, Magnis (Carvoran)

tribunus cohortis primae Aeliae Dacorum, Camboglanna (Birdoswald)

praefectus alae Petrianae, Petrianis (Stanwix)

praefectus numeri Maurorum Aurelianorum, Aballava (Burgh-by-Sands)

tribunus cohortis secundae Lingonum, Congavata (Drumburgh ?)

tribunus cohortis primae Hispanorum, Axeloduno (Castlesteads ?)

tribunus cohortis secundae Thracum, Gabrosenti (Burrow Walls)

tribunus cohortis primae Aeliae classicae, Tunnocelo (Moresby)

tribunus cohortis primae Morinorum, Glannibanta (Ravenglass)

This is the last glimpse of the army of Hadrian's Wall. Many of the units had garrisoned their forts for two centuries.

Professor E. Birley kindly allowed us access to his files for information on the units on the Wall. He is not necessarily in agreement with the conclusions set forth here.